SERMON OUTLINES

on

Heroes of Faith

Hebrews 11

Charles R. Wood

Grand Rapids, MI 49501

Sermon Outlines on Heroes of Faith: Hebrews 11

Published in 2008 by Kregel Publications, a division of Kregel, Inc., P.O. Box 2607, Grand Rapids, MI 49501.

Scripture quotations are from the King James Version of the Holy Bible.

ISBN 978-0-8254-4179-0

Printed in the United States of America

08 09 10 11 12 / 5 4 3 2 1

Contents

Introduction

The writer of Hebrews dealt with major matters of faith as they related to the integration of Jew and Gentile in a homogenous Christianity. In marshaling his arguments for the priority of faith over works, the author gathered a group of illustrations from prominent Old Testament characters. It is likely that his choice of personalities was limited to the Old Testament, at least partly because those early saints would have had an impact on the Jewish believers to whom he was writing. Whatever his motive, however, he produced in the process a marvelous chapter of Scripture that is often called the "Hebrews Hall of Fame."

These sermons on Hebrews 11 are arranged sequentially, but there is no reason they would have to be preached in any specific order. In fact, it appears that many contemporary congregations, somewhat resistant to long series of messages or lessons, prefer shorter treatments of Scripture. The messages all have the same general theme—the objectivity of the faith demonstrated by these ancient people. They all believed God enough to obey Him, follow His directions, or do His bidding.

The characters analyzed in these sermons run the gamut from the outstanding to the somewhat questionable in character, but they all have their faith in common. Thus, a brief series of messages could be constructed on the subject of faith itself, as revealed in the lives of these diverse personalities. An entirely different series could be constructed based on these people seen as Old Testament heroes. Obviously, specific sermons can be selected for solo treatment as well.

As is always the case with my messages, a single one can produce more than one sermon. Many of the individual points within a sermon can readily be expanded to stand on their own as worthwhile presentations. It is also my continual desire that the sermons be useful in stimulating thought and assisting study. The pages may be torn out of the book and used "as is," but they will be far more effective if they are translated by further study and careful consideration into the preacher's own production.

May the God of all grace grant that the products of my pulpit might be used to strengthen and expand the faith of the people of God.

CHARLES R. WOOD

That Hebrews Hall of Fame

Hebrews 10:19–12:13

Introduction:

"But now abideth faith, hope, [love], these three" (1 Cor. 13:13). And each one has its own chapter in the New Testament.

- Faith in Hebrews 11
- Hope in 1 Corinthians 15
- Love in 1 Corinthians 13

But there is much more to the Hebrews passage than what meets the eye.

I. The Context

- A. All Scripture must be considered in the light of its context
- B. General outline
  - 1. The mission of Christ
  - 2. The priesthood of Christ
- C. Specific treatment
  - 1. Begins at 10:19 with "therefore brethren"
  - 2. Because of what we have in Christ (10:20–21)
    - a. Let us
      - (1) Draw near (10:22)
      - (2) Hold fast (10:23)
      - (3) Consider one another (10:24–25)
    - b. Let us not turn back (10:26–31)
    - c. Let us remember what we have already been through (10:32–39)
    - d. Let us consider the example we have (chap. 11)
    - e. Let us hang tough no matter what (chap. 12)

II. The Challenge

- A. The key issue here is in 10:23, "Let us hold fast . . . without wavering"
  - 1. They were going through times of trial
  - 2. They were tempted to turn back
  - 3. The price of turning back was very high (10:26–31)
  - 4. They had been through trials before (10:32–34)
- B. More reasons to hold fast in trouble are provided
  - 1. There is a reward for hanging on (10:35)
  - 2. Promises are fulfilled for those who stay around to see it (10:36)
  - 3. His coming will straighten out everything (10:37)
  - 4. We are supposed to live by faith anyhow (10:38–39)

C. Chapter 11 lists people who lived by faith—many under difficult circumstances—and is designed to help believers in their trouble
D. Chapter 12 further encourages hanging on—many trials are signs of God's love and working in their lives

III. The Content

There are many faith principles in chapter 11, but there are certain ones that stand out over all.

A. An encouragement that common people can stand strong
   1. These were not all heroes in the rest of their lives
      a. A man who got drunk and committed incest
      b. A man characterized by deception
      c. A man who lied about his wife
      d. A man who murdered another
      e. A prostitute, a noted womanizer, and an adulterer
   2. You don't have to be special to have faith enough to stand
B. A demonstration of how these common people—such as Abraham—triumphed
   1. A move without a destination
   2. Acceptance of a physical impossibility
   3. The offering of an only son
C. An encouragement to hang on in the face of trouble
   1. They all went through hard times
   2. They all (mostly) made mistakes
   3. They all triumphed in the end (v. 13)
D. A challenge to do right when it is difficult or when it doesn't seem to work out
   1. They were called upon to do difficult things
   2. Sometimes things didn't work out (35–37)
   3. They all "obtained a good report"

Conclusion:

The entire passage is designed to teach how faith operates, what faith can do for us, and what faith can accomplish through us. The readers were facing hard times that were not self-created, and they were considering just giving up and turning back. The writer is encouraging them to keep on going. If they could hang in with what they faced (and if the people in chapter 11 could hang in with what they faced), then surely we can find the strength, through faith, to hang on in our situations.

You Gotta Believe

Hebrews 11:1–3

Introduction:

"You gotta believe" is a popular saying that points out what's wrong with much belief or faith. "Faith" is a nebulous and ill-defined term freely bandied about. Even Christians mess up on it. For too many it is a means of getting what you don't have. Faith is actually far broader than that!

I. The Meaning of Faith

A. Usual meaning: believing with emphasis on believing
   1. Believe hard enough and things will happen
   2. Illustrated by "positive imaging"

B. Biblical meaning: believing with emphasis on what is believed
   1. Romans 10:17: "Faith cometh by hearing, and hearing by the word of God." Faith comes as a result of hearing what God has said
   2. Supported: "Faith is the [foundation] of things hoped for" (v. 1)
      a. Faith is hope on a foundation—what God has said
      b. Differs between hope (common use) and faith: "The [conviction] of things not seen" (v. 1)
      c. The conviction that things not yet seen will be seen (supported by v. 3)
   3. Expressed: faith is hearing God, believing what God has said, and acting upon that belief
   4. Emphasis of chapter is not on what men got from God by faith but on what they did by faith—it is a record of obedience

C. Summary: Faith is believing God will likely do what He can do and will certainly do what He has promised to do sufficiently to make me do what I ought to do

II. The Manner of Faith

A. It is not a leap in the dark. It is a step in the Light

B. Everyone believes
   1. Wrong question: Do you believe? Of course!
   2. Right question: Who or what do you believe?
   3. There are all kinds of alternatives
      a. Blind chance
      b. Predetermined program

    c. Man's inherent goodness
    d. One's own strength
C. Things happen as a result of faith
  1. Don't get caught in some form of determinism
  2. "By faith"—as the result of believing God
    a. Weak, fallible men did great things
    b. The power of faith shown by contrast to rest of their lives (when they acted in faith, great things happened)

III. The Message of Faith

A. Act by faith on the basis of what He has said
  1. Obey no matter what
  2. Do what is right no matter what
B. Wait by faith for the fulfillment of His promises
  1. But don't wait by faith—and thus get disappointed—when you don't trust enough to obey
  2. We trust for salvation, why not for life?
C. Beseech by faith His intervention in life
D. Base all upon His will as revealed in the Word (you cannot separate faith from the Bible nor the Bible from faith)

Conclusion:

God has spoken; do we believe what He has said? This is the one abiding question. God has made to us exceedingly great and precious promises. Do we believe Him? If we do, then this faith is the foundation for all we hope for. It is the conviction of what we have heard but do not yet see. This faith is the opposite of sight.

Bloody Murder

Hebrews 11:4; Genesis 4:1–15

Introduction:

Speaking of Satan, Christ said in John 8:44, "He was a murderer from the beginning." He was the cause of humankind's death and the first act of killing after the Fall—murder. Satan has always been involved in killing, but this first murder is interesting.

I. It Was an Issue of Faith

- A. God must have given an unrecorded commandment
  1. Definition of faith unlocks difficult story: Faith is hearing God and believing Him enough to act on what was heard
  2. May have been declared at the "clothing" of Adam and Eve
- B. Involved the way back to God
  1. See Genesis
     - a. Creation of man
     - b. Communion with man
     - c. Fall of man
     - d. Way back to God made known
  2. God's principles of operation are eternal: "Without shedding of blood is no remission [of sin]" (Heb. 9:22)
  3. God had given a commandment—now faith would come into play

II. It Was an Issue of Division

- A. Both had same command
- B. Responses were very different
  1. Abel believed God and did what He said
  2. Cain did not believe God enough to do what He said
     - a. He was a religious man
     - b. His offering cost him more than Abel's
     - c. His way doubtlessly appeared better (especially since it cost more)
- C. A pattern was set
  1. God's way—shed blood; man's way—fruit of works
  2. Something already done; something to be done
  3. Something that cost a life; something that took some effort

D. Explains
   1. Only two ways—God's or mine
   2. Explains why men will reject the simple and embrace the costly
   3. "Nothing in my hand I bring . . ." —Augustus Toplady

III. It Was an Issue of Determination

A. In his anger at God's rejection, Cain turned to murder

B. Established a pattern
   1. Men who do it their own way are always hostile to those who do it God's way
   2. Killing in the name of religion (Note: biblical Christianity has rarely killed—more often it has been killed)

IV. It Was an Issue of Instruction

A. Abel did exactly what he was supposed to do—perfect obedience

B. The result was that he was killed
   1. He lost his life
   2. He really gained a lot
      a. Heaven
      b. Eternal reward
      c. Seed (through Seth)
      d. Everlasting good name

C. At the very beginning a great truth was revealed
   1. Faith is concerned with what God has said and not with how things work out
   2. Faith believes God enough to do right no matter the consequences
   3. Bible truth is not determined by experiences or consequences

Conclusion:

Faith hears what God has said and believes it enough to act on it. Faith considers who commanded and what was commanded. Faith doesn't consider consequences. When God says, "Do it this way," faith does it. This is the faith that saves. This is the faith that triumphs. Be careful not to get in the line of Cain.

"He Being Dead Yet Speaketh"

Hebrews 11:4

Introduction:

Abel paid with his life for his faith, but it wasn't without its benefits. Among them was the blessing of a continuing testimony. Although he has been dead for thousands of years, he continues to speak, or rather his faith continues to speak. What is it that he says?

I. He Says That Faith Is Hearing God and Believing Him Enough to Obey Him

A. Abel did so; Cain did not
B. Abel is a model of faith; Cain a model of unbelief

II. He Says There Is Only One Way to Help a Ruined Creature

A. Man ruined by the fall
B. Cast out of God's garden—main point was broken fellowship
C. Only possible restoration is through what God said
D. God's way was substitution—hits at heart of Satan's statement, "Ye shall not surely die" (Gen. 3:4)

III. He Says There Is Often a Price to Pay for Doing Right

A. Comes under "when God seems to fail" heading
B. This may be most helpful thing he says

IV. He Says the Only Difference Between Men Lies in Their Response to What God Has Said

A. Cain and Abel stood on common ground
B. Both had same command and resources
C. Faith was the only difference
D. We have many differences in mind, but God sees only one—faith

V. He Says There Is a Great Difference Between Biblical Christianity and Mere Religion

A. Biblical Christianity focuses by faith on what God has said
B. Mere religion ultimately puts its focus on what man thinks
C. No matter how much truth a system may contain, if it gives low priority to what God has said or in any way subtracts, adds, or alters, it is mere religion

D. To the degree biblical Christianity does this, it takes on the aspect of mere religion

VI. He Says the Religious Will React to the Biblical in Predictable Ways

A. Cain was angry at Abel—his real anger was with God, but he took it out on Abel
B. His problem was that Abel's faith rebuked his unbelief (hearing God and not believing Him enough to act on what He says)
C. The religious get angry at the biblical because they touch the raw nerve-end of rebellion

VII. He Says That Sincerity Means Absolutely Nothing

A. Sincerity is often made a criterion
B. It means nothing unless tied to faith
   1. Sincerity is subjective
   2. Faith is objective—based on character and communication of God

VIII. He Says That Unbelief Has an Awful Penalty

A. God exercised judgment and justice
B. Cain said that the penalty was "more than he could bear"
C. There is always a penalty for unbelief
   1. Unbelief regarding God's way of salvation—hell
   2. Unbelief regarding God's commands for living—many things

Conclusion:

Abel being dead yet speaks. What is he saying to you?

Abel: The Grave Talker

Hebrews 11:4–5

Introduction:

A voice from beyond. What does it say? Though murdered by his brother at a young age, his legacy lives on thousands of years later.

I. **The Grave Talker**
   A. Echoing through the centuries, Abel's voice can still be heard today
   B. Be sure to hear the message

II. **Setting the Stage (Gen. 4:1–10)**
   A. Birth order: Cain was the older; Abel was the younger
   B. Occupation: Cain was a farmer; Abel was a shepherd
   C. Sacrifice: Cain brought food; Abel brought an animal
   D. God's response: Cain was rejected; Abel was accepted
   E. Analysis: Cain was religious (self-effort); Abel had reality (submission)
   F. Legacy: Cain was the father of false religion; Abel was the first man of faith

III. **The Voice of the Grave Talker**
   A. Abel speaks to us clearly even though long dead
   B. He says, "Have faith enough to do life God's way"

IV. **The Questions Raised by the Grave Talker**
   A. What is the foundation of your belief system?
      1. Is it a life of works or a life of faith?
      2. The grave talker says, "Put your faith in God's plan"
   B. What is the quality of your worship practice?
      1. Is it a life in accord with biblical teaching?
      2. The grave talker says, "Give God your best, not your leftovers, and live a life of genuine sacrifice"

Conclusion:

In the earliest days of human history, a man believed God enough to obey His voice. Another man decided to do things his own way and "lost it" when his way proved to be inadequate. There is always the human tendency to do things our own way. Are you yielding to that tendency? Or do you believe God enough to do things His way?

The Man Who Wasn't

Hebrews 11:5; Genesis 5:18–24; Jude 14

Introduction:

Two men in the Bible got to do what Christ did not—they went to heaven without dying—Enoch and Elijah. We know a lot about Elijah and can understand his translation, but we don't know much about Enoch. Or do we? We know more than you may think. Notice: by faith—"as a result of" not "by means of"—Enoch was translated (did not see death) and was not found (simply disappeared). For before his translation—in his lifetime—he had this testimony that he pleased God. So we see that he pleased God by faith (Heb. 11:5) and, as a result, was translated. The big issue in his life (according to Genesis) was that he walked with God. Let's tie it all together.

I. **The Day of Enoch**
   A. He lived in a terrible day—probably worse than today. Note the indications:
      1. General downward trend from Adam to Noah
      2. The judgment of earth by the flood (Enoch lived only about 100 years before that point)
      3. The very fact a prophet was needed at this time (Jude 14)
      4. The type of people to whom he spoke—"ungodly" (Jude 15)
      5. The content of his prophecy—judgment
      6. The contrast implied by "Enoch walked with God"—others didn't
   B. His day was awful as men sped on the self-willed course that began at the foot of a tree in Eden and would soon end in a watery grave on an inundated earth

II. **The Prophecy of Enoch**
   A. Its object: The ungodly described in Jude 16
   B. Its content
      1. Second coming (at least hint of millennium)
      2. Conviction
      3. Judgment
   C. Its manner
      1. What he said is important

2. The fact that he said it is even more so
3. Here his faith begins to show—he heard what God said, believed it, acted on it (spoke)

III. The Faith of Enoch

Faith showed; in fact, he prophesied.

A. He walked with God—lived for God—in an evil world
   1. He believed God that it could be done and went and did it
   2. This is harder than preaching about it
B. His faith is both the same as and different from Abel's
   1. Abel's faith
      a. Acceptance by God
      b. Peace with God
      c. Return to God
      d. Saving
   2. Enoch's faith
      a. Acceptable to God
      b. Walk with God
      c. Live for God
      d. Living
   3. We need the faith of both men
C. The faith that pleased God and got Enoch translated
   1. Walk—he lived for God in an evil day
   2. Warn—he spoke God's message to ungodly men
   3. Wait—he placed his deposit in something beyond this world and believed God would deliver him

Conclusion:

Faith—hearing God and believing Him enough to act on it. It will get you back to God. It will enable you to live in an evil day. It will give you courage to stand. It will ultimately deliver you from the wrath to come. To say "I can't live for God" is to declare a lack of faith (see v. 6).

For Without Faith . . .

Hebrews 11:6

Introduction:

Christianity and religion are opposites. There is no greater enemy than religion—not even humanism. The key essential difference lies right here: "For without faith it is impossible . . ."

I. **What Is Faith?**
   A. This entire passage speaks of faith
   B. The basic definition: believing God enough to act on His commandments
   C. This is the main point of difference between Christianity and religion

II. **Why Is This So?**
   A. Logic demands it: "He that cometh to God must believe that he is"
      1. Initial contact with God involves belief
      2. Because God can't be seen or proved, anything having to do with God requires faith
   B. Restoration to God requires it
      1. Story of Abel
      2. If a man doesn't believe what God has said, he'll do as Cain
   C. Successful living is based on it
      1. Story of Enoch
         a. No success without obedience; no obedience without faith
         b. This is true even in a very bad day
      2. Belief in God and what He has said undergirds all
   D. Necessary tie to the future
      1. So much of Christianity always has been future
         a. For Old Testament saints
         b. For New Testament Christians
      2. Only faith can relate to the future
   E. Vital to get things from God
      1. "A rewarder of them . . ." (He becomes the One who rewards)
      2. God wants to give; He is pleased by giving
      3. There is no other way to get things for sure
   F. Summary
      1. The means of satisfaction God has chosen
         a. Puts everything on Him

(1) Salvation
(2) Sustenance
(3) Security
(4) Supply
(5) Significance

b. You can't please God without it

III. How Does It Apply?

A. Unbelief is a great hindrance
   1. Keeps from God
   2. Undermines obedience
   3. Creates fear of the future
   4. Limits reception
   5. Creates uncertainty, discouragement

B. How is belief developed?
   1. Knowledge
   2. Commitment
   3. Prayer
   4. Action

Conclusion:

Faith and belief are key elements in Christianity. How are you doing in these two areas?

Enoch: The Disappearing Man

Hebrews 11:5–6

Introduction:

Enoch and Elijah got to do something even Jesus didn't get to do—they both went to heaven without experiencing death. In the case of Enoch, we are given a specific reason why he did so—it was because he walked with God. He has several lessons to teach us as a result.

I. The Story of the Disappearing Man

A. Enoch skipped death (don't try this at home)
  1. We know no details
  2. We are simply told that "he was not because God took him"

B. Enoch pleased God
  1. This was the reason God chose to take him directly to heaven
  2. Pleasing God is a possibility for every person

II. The Question from the Disappearing Man

A. It does not have to do with discovering how to escape death

B. It does have to do with pleasing God. Wouldn't you like to have an unusual personal relationship with God?

III. The Life Lessons

A. An unusual personal relationship begins at the point of personal faith
  1. We must acknowledge God's existence
  2. We must seek God's involvement
  3. We must accept God's provision

B. An unusual personal relationship produces a powerful light in the darkness in which we live (Jude 14–15)
  1. We can stand up for God
  2. We can speak out for God

C. An unusual personal relationship is developed through a daily walk with the Lord (Gen. 5:21–24)
  1. We need a regular meeting place
  2. We need constant communication
  3. We need continually to return to the same place
  4. We need a regular review plan

Conclusion:

An unusual personal relationship with the Lord is available to everyone who knows Him. We need to pray the "shoe prayer": "Help me to take my next step with you."

By Faith: Noah

Hebrews 11:7

Introduction:

Noah is a historical character. He actually lived. He actually ran a portable zoo. As a real person, he has something to teach us.

I. The Days of Noah (Gen. 6:5–8; Matt. 24:36–39; Luke 17:26–30)

- A. Evil (Gen. 6:5)—enough to bring destructive judgment
- B. Complacent
  1. Looked good to men
  2. Self-satisfied
- C. Indifferent
  1. Whole point of Christ's reference to it
  2. No thought of impending judgment

II. The Faith of Noah: "By faith Noah . . ."

- A. Instructed by God (Gen. 6:13ff.)
  1. Told all he needed to know
  2. God tells us all we need to know
- B. Heard what God said and believed it
  1. Enough to do it (Gen. 7:5)
  2. Always a challenge to us
- C. Essence of his faith was obedience
  1. This is the essence of all faith
  2. Anyone known for faith must be known for obedience

III. The Preaching of Noah

- A. He is called a preacher (2 Peter 2:5). This is a strange term for Old Testament times
- B. He preached by action
  1. It was what he did that revealed his belief
  2. He impacted his family
- C. Note contrast between him and Lot (Luke 17:26–29)

IV. The Witness of Noah

- A. Notice the progression of the chapter
  1. Abel—peace with God
  2. Enoch—walk with God
  3. Noah—witness for God
     - a. This order is important in life
     - b. There is a danger in reversing the last two
- B. Note his obedience—he did what he was told

C. Note the meaning to the readers of Hebrews
    1. Keep hanging on (Abel, Enoch, Noah did)
    2. Explained further by the next point

V. The Results of Noah

A. The eighth person
    1. Not genealogical
    2. Just eight saved

B. He was not successful
    1. By modern standards
    2. He just did what he was supposed to do

C. He shows a principle: Faithful obedience is key

Conclusion:

To people in trouble, tempted to quit, follow the example of Noah. Find out God's will. Do it. Leave the consequences to Him. Never base your obedience on success.

Noah: Aquaman

Hebrews 11:7

Introduction:

There are all kinds of "special people" in the world of entertainment: Superman, Spiderman, even Underdog. The story of Noah could be updated by calling him "Aquaman." Noah prepared an ark for the saving of his household and thus kept mankind alive on the earth.

I. The Story of Aquaman

A. Noah is famous for the ark, the animals, and the flood

1. Imagine building a boat in a world that had never seen rain
2. Imagine the effort involved in gathering the animals
3. Imagine the patience involved in waiting for the flood to abate

B. Noah's real heartbeat in it all was his family; he saw to it that they were all on board

II. The Challenge from Aquaman

A. In contrast to Lot, all of Noah's children were on the boat when the flood came

B. Are all your children "on the boat"?

III. The Story of Noah Raises Questions About Children

A. Have all of yours personally accepted Jesus Christ as Savior?

B. Are they learning to obey and honor their parents?

C. Are they developing a real, growing relationship with God?

D. Are they beyond trusting your Christianity or walk with the Lord to be adequate for their own needs?

IV. The Story of Noah Raises Questions for Parents

A. Is spiritual leadership a passion and priority in your life?

B. Are you confronting or conforming to our mixed-up world?

C. Are you living the life of daily reality?

D. Are you modeling patient persistence in following God? Are you currently what you want your children to be someday?

Conclusion:

Parenting is not an easy task in the time in which we live. Noah shows us some important facts and raises some searching questions about the task. You can be a superhero at home! Learn from Noah.

Abraham: Man of Faith

Hebrews 11:8

Introduction:

In some ways, Abraham is one of the most important people in the Old Testament. In other ways, he is just a typical man. His life, however, is very instructive in regard to faith.

I. Abraham Was No One Special

A. Proof
1. We know nothing of his background
2. He was likely originally an idolater (Josh. 24:2; Acts 7:2)
3. He was at best a hesitant believer

B. Purpose
1. All the emphasis in the Abraham story is on God
2. This is an encouragement to us

II. Abraham Had a Clear Message from God

A. Form
1. Great detail with quite a bit of prophecy
2. But there were really no specifics
3. It all demanded great faith

B. Application
1. We have equal information
2. We have far more detail
3. We often lack specifics
4. And thus our faith is tested

III. Abraham Faced an Enormous Challenge

A. The scope of the challenge
1. Go against your background, family, and traditions
2. Move toward a totally unknown destiny
3. Stand completely alone

B. Meaning
1. We face challenges today
2. We have the same basic issues
3. What we face is nothing as difficult as that which Abraham faced

IV. Abraham Demonstrated His Faith by Obedience

A. Facts
1. Nothing is said about belief in the passage
2. The emphasis is on action—obedient action

3. There was belief, but it was only made meaningful by obedient action

B. Implications
    1. We make a big issue of belief by itself
    2. Belief is only made meaningful by obedient action
    3. Every commandment of Scripture faces us with the same situation as Abraham (only usually on a much smaller scale)

C. Obedient action is the way common men rose to dominate biblical history

V. Abraham Issues a Great Challenge to Us

A. We are often faced with strange situations
    1. God's Word is always clear, but sometimes the "Lord's leading" is a bit confusing
    2. We are often asked to do things that appear senseless or unreasonable
    3. We often must act on the basis of "inadequate" information
    4. We rarely see the end from the beginning

B. Abraham sends us a clear message
    1. We don't have to know the details if we are clear about the Lord's leading
    2. We have enough information and examples in the Bible to make us responsible for responding in faith
    3. Faith is meaningless unless it is sufficient to cause us to act
    4. You don't have to be anything special to be used of God

Conclusion:

Can you image Mrs. Abraham when Mr. Abraham came home and said, "We are moving, and I don't know where we are going"? Regardless of every other factor, Abraham did what God told him to do, and he became the father of a great nation. Do it His way. He may have something special in store for you.

Abraham: The Bionic Man

Hebrews 11:8–19

Introduction:

We heard much in the '70s about the "bionic man" who was capable of super-human feats because of the way he had been engineered . . . or reengineered. The phenomenal life of Abraham, when viewed in the light of the day in which he lived, would almost make him look "bionic."

I. The Life Lesson from the Bionic Man

A. Your spiritual journey isn't about perfection

B. Your spiritual journey is about direction

II. The Secret of Bionic Living

A. Abraham had bionic ears (v. 8)

1. He repeatedly heard the voice of God speaking to him in specific ways
2. Are you listening for God, even through the noise of life?

B. Abraham had bionic feet (v. 8)

1. Whenever he got orders from God, he moved in that direction immediately and unconditionally
2. Are you following God's directions immediately and unconditionally?

C. Abraham had bionic eyes (v. 10)

1. He was able to see what others were unable to see
2. Are you viewing life from an eternal perspective? Are you "looking for a city"?

D. Abraham had a bionic mouth (vv. 13–14)

1. He spoke his convictions openly
2. Are you sure of your heavenly destination and willing to speak of it?

E. Abraham had bionic hands (v. 17)

1. God said, "Give me your son." Abraham then used what he already had available
2. Are you releasing everything nearest and dearest to you?

Conclusion:

Bionic living is nothing more than taking simple steps of radical commitment. God is in the business of turning imperfect people into supernatural forces for His kingdom. Will you be one of them?

By Faith

Hebrews 11:9

Introduction:

Abraham was a real person. Three events are singled out of his very eventful life: his call out of his homeland, his sojourn in the land of promise, and his test in regard to Isaac.

Faith is not something subjective and ethereal; it is firmly based on God's Word and obedience to it. The second issue in the life of Abraham as identified by the writer of Hebrews breaks down into three parts.

I. Abraham Sojourning

"By faith he sojourned in the land of promise, as in a strange country, dwelling in tabernacles [tents] . . ." (Heb. 11:9).

- A. This was another act of faith
  1. "The Canaanites were in the land" (Gen. 12:6)
  2. He heard God and believed that this land would be his
  3. What a contrast with spies later (Num. 13:32–33)
- B. In tents
  1. He was not used to this existence; he was not a nomad but a city dweller prior to God's call
  2. Emphasizes the idea of sojourning or dwelling temporarily
  3. Points to an obvious impermanence—he knew the land wasn't his but would be someday
- C. His humanity shows
  1. He went into Egypt in the face of famine
  2. He lied about his wife
     - a. Each time he showed lack of faith—incongruous
     - b. He was just like us—we trust God for salvation but can't trust Him enough to be obedient in life

II. Abraham Separating

- A. Once sojourning established (temporary home), then separation (setting apart) is inevitable (because the sojourner has a different destination, etc.)
- B. Illustrated in Abraham's life with Lot—Lot walked by sight (Gen. 13:10)
  1. He beheld (13:10)
  2. He chose (13:11)
  3. He journeyed (13:11)

4. He dwelt (13:12)
5. He pitched toward (13:12)
6. He dwelt (note second use and contrast) (14:12)
7. He became part of culture (19:1)
8. He shared in its calamity (19:17)

C. Important contrast
1. The man who walks by faith sees things as God says they are
2. The man who walks by sight sees things as they appear to be
3. Thus
    a. It takes more faith to walk by sight, seeing things as they appear to be, than to walk by faith, seeing things as God says they are
    b. Two kinds of men will see things very differently
    c. Settling the issue of destination settles the issue of separation

III. Abraham Seeking: "For he looked for a city . . ." (Heb. 11:10)

A. He looked for a city
1. He heard about it from God
2. Believed it in spite of Canaanites, tents, Egypt, Lot, etc.
3. Even believed it though he sensed it would transcend generations (our problem is often haste)

B. He saw beyond his own time
1. If God said it, it had to happen
2. Puts our faith to shame—if we don't see it or at least see how it could happen, we get all bent out of shape

C. Details given
1. A well-founded city
2. Designed and built by God
3. He saw this from the very start

Conclusion:

Abraham had settled some issues. He was a sojourner, on the way from one place to another, and this involved a necessary separation. He was also a seeker, with his faith resting on what God had said rather than on when it would come to pass.

So what do we need to learn from Abraham? First, we are sojourners. This will result in separation and make that truth much clearer and the task much easier. Second, we need to seek what God has promised and trust Him for it even though it may not be evident when it will come—if He has said it, it will come.

The Faith of Sarah

Hebrews 11:11–12

Introduction:

The Hebrews record now comes to another character, and this one is a woman. She figures prominently in the life of Abraham. She teaches us even more about faith.

I. The Story

Note the way it progresses in Genesis.

A. Promise given (12:2–3)
B. Promise repeated—added details (13:14–18)
C. Promise reconfirmed—more detail (15:1–6ff.)
D. Hagar incident (16:1–4)
E. Specifics introduced (17:1–8, 15–22)
F. Sarah included for first time (18:9–15)
G. Actual fulfillment recorded (21:1–8)

II. The Details

A. There's a marked change here
   1. Sarah does nothing by way of action
   2. She is the first one who does nothing
   3. Her story deals with faith as we usually define it; she just believed what God told her
B. There is an ever-present element here
   1. Traces to Eve and the first giving of the promise regarding Messiah
   2. Purpose of God ever in view—messianic promise
   3. The giving of the child had to come to pass
C. The element of laughter
   1. Abraham laughed (Gen. 17:17). His laughter was likely unbelieving
   2. Sarah laughed (18:12) likely to herself. Some measure of unbelief because of rebuke
   3. God made Sarah to laugh: "You laughed before, you can really laugh now"
D. This is a turning point for Abraham
   1. Very unbelieving before this—didn't really believe promise
   2. He was so unbelieving that he wanted Ishmael elevated (note the trouble that caused)
   3. Seems birth of son changed all this (same man who laughed is now willing to sacrifice)

4. Once he had received this promise, he was never the same again. Oh, that we could learn thus from God's provisions

III. The Lessons

A. The basis for faith

1. What God has said is so
2. What God says will come to pass, will come to pass
3. What God has promised will surely happen
4. God is able to do anything (Gen. 18:14), and His promise is never impossible

B. Believing faith necessary for accomplishment

1. Notice "because" she believed
2. Even in regard to some promises of God

C. The danger of helping God accomplish His work

1. Fine balance involved here
2. Most obvious in salvation
3. Don't violate the promise in an effort to make it come to pass
4. Big danger is in violating commandment (doing wrong to help God keep His promises)

Conclusion:

It must have been strange for Sarah once again. The initial move was doubtlessly strange. The promise of the child to an old woman must have been strange. The birth of the child must have been even more strange. What God has promised, however, He will surely do! Our part? Only believe!

Not Having Received the Promises

Hebrews 11:13–16

Introduction:

There are many things that New Testament believers possess that were not the property of Old Testament saints. The writer of Hebrews expressed that fact by stating that they all died in faith but without having actually received the promises. There are many ways in which the faith of these Old Testament saints is superior to that of those who have lived after the crucifixion and resurrection.

I. Old Testament Salvation (v. 13)

- A. These all died in faith
  1. Those mentioned previously
  2. Could read "in the faith"
- B. They had not received the promises
  1. The promises were yet future
  2. Their view of the future was rather vague ("afar off")
- C. They embraced the promises by faith
  1. They were assured of them
  2. They took them to themselves
  3. They had a different viewpoint as a result ("strangers and pilgrims")
- D. This is the essence of Old Testament faith
  1. They had confidence in the promises and provision of God
  2. They were saved by faith in a God that would do what was needed for their salvation

II. Old Testament Demonstration (v. 14)

- A. Old Testament saints did not demonstrate their faith by religious observance
  1. They, doubtlessly, faithfully kept the law
  2. That observance, however, was not the crux of their testimony
- B. A life of faith revealed their righteousness
  1. They sought a homeland beyond Palestine
  2. They demonstrated righteousness by living by faith

III. Old Testament Anticipation (vv. 15–16)

- A. They demonstrated a forward look

   1. They were free to return (literally and figuratively) to the countries they had left
   2. They didn't even think about those options that were open to them
B. They looked for something specific
   1. They desired a better country
   2. That desired country was somewhere beyond this earth
C. Their anticipation and faith gained them great blessings
   1. They became, in the truest sense, the people of God
   2. They have a prepared "city" waiting for them

Conclusion:

All saints—both Old and New Testament—are saved by faith. All saints should live by faith as the Old Testament saints did. All saints should have the focus of Old Testament saints: those who are "strangers and pilgrims on the earth" and who desire that anticipated city.

By Faith: Abraham

Hebrews 11:17–19

Introduction:

There are three incidents in the life of Abraham mentioned in Hebrews 11. The first is his call out of Ur. The second involves his "sojourn" in the land of promise. The third has to do with his offering of Isaac. This message looks at the third of these—the offering of Isaac. There is much more here than meets the eye, as so much of Abraham's overall relationship to God is tied up in this situation.

I. The Background of the Story

- A. The promise of God to Abraham (Gen. 12:1–3)
  1. Abraham would be involved in becoming a great nation
  2. Abraham was already old and had no child
- B. Gift of Isaac is another part of the story as well
  1. There were repeated promises and exchanges between Abraham, Sarah, and God, yet Sarah was well beyond childbearing years
  2. Isaac was a special gift and absolutely essential to the fulfillment of the promise of God
- C. The command to offer up Isaac (Gen. 22:1–14)
  1. Directly given to Abraham by God
  2. Ran counter to everything that Abraham knew of God's dealings with men
  3. Abraham was absolutely sure of what God had said to him
  4. Don't get hung up on the details as they are hypothetical because of God's direct intervention

II. The Response of Abraham

- A. Note the tenses of the verbs in the passage
  1. Had "offered up Isaac" (Heb. 11:17)
  2. "Offered up his only begotten son" (v. 17)
- B. Note the reminder of the promises located in him
  1. "His only begotten son" (v. 17)
  2. "Of whom it was said, that in Isaac shall thy seed be called" (v. 18)
- C. Note the background of his response (it doesn't lessen enormity, but it does explain)
  1. He believed that God was able to raise him from the dead (v. 19)

2. Believed so strongly that it was the same as if he had received him back from the dead

III. The Lessons of the Account

A. Abraham's belief teaches so much
   1. His attitude was, "If God says it, do it"
   2. Surely he didn't understand how the whole thing could work out
   3. He believed God completely
      a. If God commanded it, it couldn't be wrong, and it had to work out somehow
      b. He left the working out to God. His was to obey; it was God's to work out

B. Fleshes out picture of Abraham here
   1. Three incidents teach three truths
      a. Surest place (most secure) is God's appointed place for us
      b. Walking by faith is seeing things as they actually are (sojourning)
      c. God's commands make sense—whether or not we see how
   2. Abraham rebukes the success orientation of today's Christianity
      a. Note the things he is remembered for
      b. These things could not be stressed today (so this is a book of testimonials)
   3. Note the tie in of faith and obedience again
      a. This is action again
      b. It is action based on faith (believing God enough to do what He says—and this may be the ultimate illustration)

C. Explains the concept expressed in James 2:17–26
   1. This passage has caused so much confusion
   2. The works referred to there are not good deeds (which really prove nothing; they can be easily counterfeited)
   3. The works James refers to—at least in speaking of Abraham—are acts of obedience, the obedience of faith

Conclusion:

We are not called to do what Abraham was called to do. We have simple commands. Our obedience to them shows the genuineness of our faith.

Jacob's Faith

Hebrews 11:21

Introduction:

Here is another verse that appears brief and barren but which contains much teaching. In verse 21 we see how faith overcomes the world. We also see the key to victorious faith. In this verse we see another aspect of the many-faceted jewel called faith.

I. Jacob's Blessing

A. Translation: "By faith, when he was about to die, Jacob blessed each of the sons of Joseph"

B. The story is in Genesis 48

C. What is significant?

1. Jacob reversed the blessing order
2. Joseph tried to correct it
3. Jacob refused to be swayed

D. What is involved

1. Jacob had heard from God as to what God wanted
2. Jacob would not change what God wanted
3. Jacob would not yield to the entreaties of his favorite son, Joseph

E. What this teaches

1. Faith believes God enough to do what He says no matter what
2. Faith believes God enough to go against what man wants
   a. Accounts for standing against the pressure of men (fear of man)
   b. Fear of man may not be as dangerous as love for man's approval
3. Faith overcomes the power of the flesh; it also overcomes the pressures of man

II. Jacob Worshipping

A. Translation: "and worshipped, leaning [for support] on the top of his staff" (Heb. 11:21)

B. The story is in Genesis 47:27–31

C. What is significant?

1. Jacob would not be buried in Egypt
2. Jacob accepted the promises even though he knew he would not see them
3. Faith had won out in the life of Jacob

a. What's in a name? Notice the two names used for him
b. Typical throughout his life
   (1) Jacob was the supplanter
   (2) He struggled in birth
   (3) He struggled for birthright and secured it
   (4) He struggled for blessing and secured it
   (5) He struggled with Laban for daughters and won
   (6) He struggled with Laban for cattle and won
   (7) He was ready to struggle with Esau for forgiveness
c. Then God takes over (Gen. 32)
   (1) The struggler loses
   (2) He carries a lifetime reminder
   (3) There is doubtlessly a continuing struggle
   (4) He now is "leaning on his staff [or bed]"—he is old and he has finally learned
d. He worshipped God; God has now won and Jacob—Israel—is willing to accept by faith what God has said

III. The Relationship Between the Blessing and the Worship

A. Jacob could bless according to God's direction because he had settled the issue of God's sovereignty in his life
B. We will always have trouble with faith—the battle of the flesh and the fear of man—until we come to the place of ceasing the struggle and accepting the will of God
C. Faith hears what God says and does it even though the fear—and the love—of man may say otherwise

Conclusion:

Once you have settled who is in charge in your life, you will have much less trouble with the faith that obeys and clings to the promises.

By Faith: The Bones of Joseph

Hebrews 11:22

Introduction:

If you can keep your head when all about are losing theirs, either you don't understand the situation or you know something no one else knows. Joseph always kept his head because he knew some things others didn't know.

I. The Commendable Life of Joseph

A. Trustworthy life in youth
B. Patient bearing of horrendous affliction
C. Complete lack of bitterness
D. Exceptional skills
E. Tender care of his family

II. The Incident Chosen to Exemplify His Faith

A. The oath concerning his bones (Gen. 50:24–25)
B. Why was this chosen above others?
   1. Definition of faith in Hebrews 11
   2. Showed some things Joseph knew
   3. Gives us some clue as to how he handled other events

III. What Joseph Knew

A. God's promise to Abraham (Gen. 15:13–14), Jacob's confirmation (48:21–22), and this is Joseph's response
B. Promise only partially fulfilled—no affliction yet
C. Joseph believed the promise and acted on it—wanted his bones where the action would be
D. Shows
   1. He knew what God had promised
   2. He knew God's promise would stand
   3. He knew the outworking was God's business
   4. He knew there was a bigger dimension in life—he obviously believed in eternal life—even if in a primitive way

IV. What This Explains

A. Throws light on his entire life
   1. Knew what God had promised (37:5–10)
   2. Knew God's promise would stand
   3. Knew outworking was God's business
   4. Knew there were bigger (unseen) dimensions in life

B. Explains the decision at his death
   1. Normal Egyptian treatment—embalming and entombment
   2. Chose to forgo that
   3. Overcame natural tendencies and desires

V. **What This Teaches Us**
   A. By faith, as here defined, we can overcome natural tendencies
   B. What has been promised will come to pass
   C. We need to hold on to promises
      1. We tend to set timetable, manner, and results
      2. Faith
         a. Hears Word
         b. Believes it
         c. Acts on it regardless

Conclusion:

The reason this incident was chosen is likely because of what it showed—the secret of Joseph's entire life and how we need to learn the same secret.

The Product of a Dysfunctional Family

Hebrews 11:22

Introduction:

Joseph is listed as one of the heroes of the faith in Hebrews 11. His faith was especially shown by his determination not to be buried in Egypt. He knew—by faith—that Egypt was not Israel's final home. He wanted to be "with his people." Joseph's entire life, however, was a life of faith, and it is amazing in the light of a number of negative factors, not the least of which was his family background.

I. **The Reality of Unhappy Families**
   A. Many have personal experiences
   B. It is a common experience

II. **The Story of Joseph's Dysfunctional Family**
   A. His father Jacob—"Deceiver"
      1. He is now aging, but there has been a pattern of deception
      2. He was at best a passive father (Gen. 34:1–2)
         a. He showed anger (Gen. 34:30)
         b. He did nothing when he should have acted (Gen. 35:21–22)
   B. His brothers were lustful, unruly, deceitful, vengeful
      1. Six of them were by Leah
      2. Four were by handmaids
      3. They were wild and ungoverned (Gen. 37:2–4)
      4. They were deeply cruel—they threw Joseph into a pit to die, and then sat down and ate a meal (Gen. 37:23–25)
   C. Joseph
      1. He was the only child of his mother
      2. He had a touch of arrogance when younger (shown by the sharing of his dreams)
      3. He was favored by his father
         a. The son of favorite wife, born in old age
         b. He was different from brothers
         c. He was surely the easiest to raise
      4. He was bereft of mother when young

III. **The Record of Joseph's Life**
   A. He rose to the top everywhere he was
      1. Potiphar's house

        2. In the prison
        3. Over all of Egypt
    B. He is just a notch below Daniel as described in Scripture
    C. He shows some incredible characteristics (e.g., forgiveness)
    D. In the truest sense, he lived by faith—he could not have made it through all he survived without believing that God would keep the promise of his young dreams

IV. The Lessons of Joseph's Story

A. Your life is not determined by your childhood—good or bad
B. Your life is not limited by your childhood
C. Your life will be colored by your childhood
D. Your life may be enhanced by your childhood and the choice is yours

Conclusion:

Just because things were good . . . Just because things were bad . . . It is time to come to terms with your childhood—by faith—no matter what it was like.

The Faith of Moses' Parents

Hebrews 11:23

Introduction:

There are those who believe that we must obey government no matter what. This is not the teaching of Scripture (Acts 5:29). There are frequent biblical examples of disobedience. Here's one.

I. **The Principal Actors in the Story**
   A. From the way it is written it appears to be Moses (he will be the hero of three incidents)
   B. Actually, it deals with the parents of Moses (about whom we don't know very much)

II. **The Background of the Story (Exod. 1:7–2:10)**
   A. Joseph is dead
   B. Jews begin to multiply rapidly—note wording of 1:7
   C. A Pharaoh arises who "knew not Joseph"
      1. Period of upheaval in Egypt
      2. Somehow connected with Hyksos kings
      3. A completely new dynasty comes on the throne
   D. New Pharaoh (likely already threatened) is very paranoid about Jews
   E. Policies are established to eliminate the threat they posed

III. **The Motivation of Pharaoh**
   A. This was the first but not the last time an attempt was made to eliminate Jews
      1. In book of Esther
      2. At time of birth of Christ
      3. Hitler was a modern example
   B. Reason was simple but not the whole picture—there was a force and power behind Pharaoh and all other attempts on the Jews—Satan
   C. Why were early attempts thwarted but not Hitler? It is likely involved with the fact that the Messiah had not yet come

IV. **The Actual Story**

The chronology is very important here—all this established in the mind of God before the wedding and decision to have a baby.

   A. The couple gets married
   B. They decide to have a baby

C. The baby is born
D. They hear something from God about the baby and what to do about it
E. The baby is recognized as the object of the revelation
F. They preserve the baby
   1. First at home—with difficulty
   2. Then place baby in river
   3. Baby found and taken to Pharaoh's home

V. What We Can See Here

A. The ability and willingness of God to turn things around
   1. They did what they had been told
   2. Pharaoh raised the one who would throw off his yoke
   3. A few tears were the means of turning a world upside down
   4. Just relax when you realize God is on the throne
B. Faith establishes the priorities of obedience
   1. We live in a world where priorities conflict
   2. Sometimes we don't know what to do when commands appear to overlap or contradict each other
   3. It establishes a simple priority system—obey God rather than man—no question about it
C. Faith delivers from fear of anything
   1. No evidence that they were afraid at all
   2. They had more to lose than possible to express
   3. Faith doesn't fear the consequences; faith doesn't even consider the consequences (don't go wild with this principle—restrict it strictly to the Word of God)

Conclusion:

The Bible is supreme. We ought to obey it strictly. Don't let fear deter you.

The Faith of Moses

Hebrews 11:24–26

Introduction:

The world has an enormous appeal; don't ever forget it. The appeal comes through so many different forms: the siren song of supple sexual seduction; the pounding pulse of potential power; the maddening magnetism of monarch money. It is not easy to stand against it. Somehow, Moses managed to do so.

I. The Crisis of Moses (v. 24)

A. "When he was come to years"
   1. May mean "when he was become great"
   2. Was at least forty

B. He had been adopted by Pharaoh's daughter

C. He possibly was in line for the throne—great power at least

D. He had every positive: personal fame, wealth, power, ease

E. He could have greatly reversed trends for Israel and greatly eased its suffering

F. It must have been an enormous pull for him

II. The Choice of Moses (v. 25)

A. Chose to reject elevation through identification

B. Chose to go with Israel

C. He knew the price of choice and went against every intelligent consideration

III. The Criteria of Moses (v. 26)

A. He must have had information from God
   1. His faith would almost assure that fact
   2. "Pleasure of sin for a season"—He could have been identified with Egypt and not sinned unless that choice would have gone against what he knew he should do

B. He knew what he was getting into
   1. There is a reference to Christ here
   2. He recognized the significance of an eventual reward and weighed that reward against the sacrifice

IV. The Challenge of Moses

A. Faith that trusts God to work things out

1. He was not always perfect in this regard—slaying the Egyptian
2. It has been suggested that he may not have been wrong in doing so—it may have been a sign to the people that they refused to recognize

B. Faith that overcomes the pull of the world
1. The world is always there
2. There are always rationalizations (I can make more money for the Lord's work, etc.)
3. The commandment (principle) always makes the difference
4. The only way we will stand is to weigh things as they really are
5. If this life is all there is, then go ahead and do things your way

Conclusion:

Faith hears what God says and believes it enough to act upon it. Not only in specific prohibitions of sin but also in such issues as: "Seek ye first the kingdom of God" (Matt. 6:33) and "What shall it profit a man, if he shall gain the whole world, and lose his own soul?" (Mark 8:36).

By Faith: Moses Forsook

Hebrews 11:27

Introduction:

We have seen Moses overcome the pull of the world as he renounced his place as the son of Pharaoh's daughter. He was able to walk away from the place of prominence and pleasure, etc. Moses ultimately came to the place of living a "victorious life"—there is such a thing—and we can learn from him how we might have such purpose ourselves.

I. The Event in View

A. Usually tied to Moses' flight recorded in Exodus 2:14–15

B. We need to reevaluate situation there for the reason he looked all around before acting

C. Not likely the proper place to look

1. In the passage above he fled in fear
2. In the Hebrews passage he forsook in faith

D. This most likely has reference to his final departure from Egypt in Exodus 12–14

II. The Events Involved

A. Contest with Pharaoh

1. Ten miracles
2. Four phases in the development of the request of Pharaoh
    a. Worship God in the land (8:25)
    b. Not very far away (8:28)
    c. Only the men should go (10:11)
    d. Leave flocks and herds (10:24)
3. Moses refused every compromise

B. What he faced

1. Going from the known to the unknown
2. Going from something to nothing
3. Going from security to insecurity

C. Moses made his final break with Egypt with great reluctance

1. Because of the many factors involved
2. It took "faith" to cause him to forsake

D. There is no record, however, that he ever desired to go back. Everyone else did, but he never did

1. There was a constant struggle over this

2. Moses was steadfast. When he forsook, he relinquished

III. The Lessons for Us

A. We overcome the struggle with the world by faith
1. There is a struggle for us with the world (Egypt is always a picture of the world)
2. We can never settle for less than what God has settled upon, but we are always tempted to do so
3. The only way to win the final victory is to insist on God's way in the matter

B. We overcome the fear of the unknown by faith
1. For most, the unknown is frightening (unless it is an unknown we have chosen)
2. Moses went into the unknown with a burden
3. Faith views the unknown in God's will as plainer than the known out of God's will

C. We keep from turning back by faith
1. There is a constant pull to turn back
2. Faith will not allow us to turn back
3. Faith is the only thing that will keep us—Moses had burned his bridges

D. We win the battle over separation by faith
1. It is an unending struggle
2. Satan uses the same appeals that Pharaoh used
3. We win only by Hebrews 11 faith—hearing what God has said and believing it enough to act on it no matter what

Conclusion:

Moses was able to turn his back on the court of Pharaoh (representing the world) by faith. He was able to settle the issue of separation by faith. He settled the issue once and for all that he would be completely what God wanted him to be rather than trying to accommodate to Pharaoh's enticements. Moses overcame the pull of the world and settled the issue of separation by faith—so can we!

Faith Overcoming Obstacles

Hebrews 11:28

Introduction:

When understood in the light of their historical context, many Old Testament saints stand out in brilliant relief. They were giants in the midst of pygmies. They were knowledgeable in a day of ignorance. They were spiritual in a day of superstition. The most interesting thing about them, however, may be that they are so relevant.

I. The Passage

A. "[Moses] kept the passover" means that he instituted it (v. 28)

B. The word translated "kept" should be repeated twice in the passage
  1. By faith he instituted the Passover
  2. By faith he instituted the sprinkling of blood

C. With the result being that he who destroyed the firstborn should not touch them

D. Why was this incident chosen out of the life of Moses, and what is it designed to teach us?

II. The Past

We need to see an incident in Moses' past to fully understand what is in view here.

A. God called Moses to deliver His people (Exod. 3:15–22)

B. Moses didn't want the job! This is shown by arguments with God
  1. The people won't accept me (4:1)
  2. I can't speak properly (4:10)

C. There doubtlessly were reasons behind his unwillingness to serve
  1. He saw it as impossible
  2. He didn't want the hassle with Pharaoh
     a. He knew Pharaoh well (after all, he grew up in Pharaoh's home)
     b. He was assured of God about what he was facing
  3. He also saw overwhelming responsibility down the road
     a. He knew Israel would look to him as leader
     b. He likely didn't want the responsibility (he also knew the Israelites very well)

    c. He had balked at an overwhelming task in the past

III. The Passover (Exod. 12:1–28)

A. He was given full details by God
   1. Passover observance
   2. Death of firstborn
   3. Spoliation of Egypt
   4. Moving night
B. He knew this was an absolutely crucial issue
   1. The lives of all the firstborn hung in the balance
   2. The departure of Israel was at stake
C. He managed to get the people to follow his leadership
   1. In the light of the deteriorating situation in Egypt
   2. He got them to do all kinds of details on moving night
   3. He even got them to do something seemingly pointless, like sprinkling blood on the doorposts
D. He was able to successfully complete what he had backed away from earlier

IV. The Possibility

A. The difference between his earlier reticence and his latter success was growth, and the cause of the growth was faith
B. His faith had grown in the process of the hard time before Pharaoh, which must have been exhausting
C. He now understood—faith is hearing what God says and believing Him enough to act on it even in the face of enormous obstacles

V. The Point

A. These incidents from the life of Moses show
   1. Faith overcoming the pull of the world
   2. Faith overcoming the attachment of the world (separation)
   3. Faith overcoming the obstacles of the impossible task or situation
B. This is often replicated in modern situations
   1. We have financial or other needs
   2. Our situations become impossible or are untenable
   3. But we keep going because of an understanding of the Word

Conclusion:

What are you facing that is impossible? If you are in the will of God on it, keep on going by faith (hearing the Word and believing God enough to keep on acting on it).

Isn't That About the Silliest Thing You Have Ever Heard?

Hebrews 11:30

Introduction:

Be careful of this one—it looks on the surface like the walls of Jericho exercised faith in order to fall down. Actually, the passage is speaking about the children of Israel (introduced in v. 29). Here is another example of faith designed to help us keep from falling away in the face of trials and difficulties.

I. **The History (Josh. 6)**
   A. Joshua's military genius—he was no fool coming out of the wilderness, stumbling along without purpose or plan
   B. The difficulty of the situation
      1. Just coming out of the wilderness—they had not done much fighting there and were relatively inexperienced
      2. They had no plan to fall back upon—this was an absolutely vital military campaign
   C. The geographic factors
      1. People of that time lived in or around a city and fled to it in time of trouble
      2. Jericho was a small but populous, well-fortified city that occupied a strategic location
   D. The strategy that was adopted
      1. Children of Israel were told to march around the city once each day and seven times on the seventh day
      2. They were told to shout on signal on the final day (likely had nothing to do with the walls falling down; it was rather an expression of victory)
      3. Would not really have seemed too strange to the people in Jericho to have Israel marching around their city for seven days
         a. They already knew about Israel—especially the divine intervention side (Rahab is witness to this)
         b. They knew little or nothing about Israel's religion
         c. They were likely highly superstitious people

d. They probably thought Israel was exercising some form of voodoo or witchcraft
4. Children of Israel would have found this an exceedingly strange approach
    a. They were a cosmopolitan people who had recently become familiar with warfare
    b. They were not at all superstitious
    c. They would likely have made themselves vulnerable with this approach
5. Rather obvious to us what God was trying to do (but not to the Israelites)
    a. Establishing that they could do nothing without His help
    b. Showing His mighty ability to conquer
    c. Scaring the daylights out of the rest of the people they would have to fight against

II. The Principle Involved

A. Illustrating a faith that is hearing what God says and believing enough to act upon it
B. Hebrews 11 deals with the faith that operates in the face of various situations
    1. Moses showed faith overcoming
        a. Temptation to accept world's endorsement
        b. The allure and appeal of the world
        c. The difficulty of leading others
    2. Israel at the Red Sea showed faith by plunging into the unknown when there was potential danger
C. This is a story of faith facing the seemingly foolish, foolhardy, and ridiculous on the basis of "God said it, I believe it, I will do it"

III. The Implications Developed

A. The Bible is always practical ("if it isn't practical, it isn't biblical")
    1. This is a true statement that is subject to limitations—the Bible is practical, but we don't always recognize that practicality
    2. Major caution—don't decide the Bible on the basis of what you think is practical (tendency to try to prove the Bible by the results)
B. We must obey what the Bible says even though it appears foolish or impractical
    1. Regarding some commands, there is no way they will work

2. We can learn not to try to operate the church like a business (operate it in a businesslike manner but not as a business)

Conclusion:

The approach to the conquest of Jericho must have appeared utterly foolish to the children of Israel. There are many commandments in the Word of God that appear equally foolish to us (and impossible to keep as well). God, however, is still in the business of intervening in the affairs of human beings and of making that intervention very obvious. If He says it, it can be done because He will support it.

The Faith of Rahab

Hebrews 11:31

Introduction:

Rahab finds a place in the genealogy of Christ (one of four women, three with moral problems and the other a foreigner). What distinguished this Canaanite harlot's faith to the degree that she would be included in the "Hebrews Hall of Fame"?

I. The Story (Josh. 2)

A. Two sets of spies in Old Testament
   1. They spied out Canaan in Numbers
   2. They spied out Jericho in Joshua

B. Spying out Jericho in preparation for conquest

C. The spies go to house of Rahab
   1. Likely a place to go with little chance of detection
   2. She harbors them
   3. The authorities come seeking
   4. She hides the spies
      a. Diverts the authorities
      b. Helps the spies to escape
   5. She works out an agreement with them (2:12–13)
      a. They prearrange a sign with her
      b. The binding of a scarlet thread in her window

D. Agreement kept—deliverance provided (6:22–23)
   1. Not sure of time
   2. Probably prior to laying siege (because of 6:1)

II. The Details

A. Don't get hung up on the harlot aspect
   1. Her faith is commended, not her character
   2. She is proof that anyone can come to faith and that anyone who comes is included

B. Fulfillment of an earlier prophecy
   1. Statement in Exodus 15 (Moses' Song of Deliverance)
   2. Take Exodus 15:14–16 with Joshua 2:9–11

C. An illustration of how seeking light leads to more light
   1. She had heard and was impressed
   2. Further light provided by God (in person of two spies)
   3. She sought further knowledge (deliverance agreement)
   4. It was provided (deliverance)

D. Significance of scarlet thread (rope)
   1. Color coincidental?
   2. Don't make too much of it

III. The Principle

A. Why is this here?
   1. Her receiving the spies with peace showed faith
      a. She had heard of what God had done (Josh. 2:10–11)
      b. Faith is hearing God and believing Him enough to act on what He says
   2. She acted on what God said in the face of family, friends, culture

B. A principle is thus illustrated: faith hears God, believes Him, and acts even against family, friends, culture, etc. This is a most difficult area (Matt. 10:34–35)
   1. It is difficult to go against family in regard to salvation, Christian living, and child rearing, but the answer is to hear God and believe Him enough to act in spite of family
   2. It is difficult to go against friends
   3. It is even more difficult to go against one's culture

C. This is the problem many have with a biblical lifestyle—it is countercultural
   1. The only answer—hear what God says and believe Him enough to do it
   2. Do it in spite of
      a. Family (Matt. 10:37)
      b. Friends
      c. Culture (1 John 2:15)

Conclusion:

The Jews of Jesus' time were feeling family and cultural pressure. The writer of Hebrews says only faith will keep you around. Some of you feel the same pressure. Only faith will keep you around, but it must be Hebrews 11 faith.

Gideon and the Word of God

Hebrews 11:32

Introduction:

The last section of this chapter is a summary of many other heroes of the faith. It almost seems as if the author ran out of time. He lists several names and then lists a number of accomplishments (some were done by more than one person). Gideon stands out. Let's see why.

I. The Story of Gideon (Judg. 6–7)

A. Best known for two things
1. The fleece
2. The choice of men for an army by the way they drank

B. Obviously much more to his story
1. He lived at a time of Midianite oppression
2. God called him to overthrow the Midianites
3. Gideon recoils because of weakness
4. God gives him assurance through fleece
5. Gideon calls for an army
6. God tells him the army is too large (this is explained by the fact that God wanted them to know that they didn't win on their own)
7. Gideon used the drinking process as a final test (those who scooped water showed alertness)
8. Gideon went against Midianites who got confused and turned the battle against themselves (as a result of the approach that gave them the impression they were up against a much larger force)

II. The Story Behind the Story

A. God spoke to Gideon twelve times and said twelve things to him
1. Seven in Judges 6, and all of these had to do with God preparing him for the task
   a. Verse 12—got his attention
   b. Verse 14—pointed out his weakness
   c. Verse 16—showed him His strength
   d. Verse 18—assured him of His patience
   e. Verse 20—set him up for a miracle
   f. Verse 23—reassured him
   g. Verse 25—got him started

2. Five in Judges 7, and all of these things had to do with the actual task God had given him
    a. Verse 2—tells him why to cut the army down
    b. Verse 4—still dissatisfied with army
    c. Verse 5—gives test of drinking
    d. Verse 7—assures him of victory
    e. Verse 9—reassures him of His intention to give the victory

B. Faith is hearing what God has said and believing Him enough to act on what He has commanded. Gideon did so even in the face of what appeared to be suicide

III. The Lessons of Gideon

A. The emphasis is on God's communication with Gideon
  1. God spoke to him repeatedly
  2. He had a tremendous amount of information from God
  3. He acted strictly on what he knew

B. Notice the lessons of this passage
  1. God starts with the preparation of the man before He moves to the accomplishment of the task He has for the man. This gives a new view of trials—He may be preparing you for a purpose
  2. When a man is prepared, then the performance is relatively easy. Our problem is that we try to do too much without proper spiritual preparation. That's why the Christian life is so hard
  3. The word of the Lord played a vital role in both his preparation and performance. If we are ever to accomplish great feats of faith (either believing or obedient faith), we must be people of the Word
    a. If you are having trouble doing what you know you should do, spend time in the Word
    b. If you are having trouble getting what you need from the Lord, spend time in the Word
  4. In the Bible, we have a more sure word of prophecy than even Gideon

Conclusion:

Gideon accomplished much (show from later verses) by the word of the Lord. You are never going to accomplish much by faith until the Word of the Lord has more place, impact, and effect.

The Faith of Barak

Hebrews 11:32

Introduction:

One of the most interesting and problematic stories of Scripture is placed right here. It contains all the elements necessary for fairly good fiction: a chicken-hearted man, a dynamic woman, and a gal who could drive a tent peg.

But it is all true and touches on a hot-button issue today: the role of women in Christianity.

I. The Story of Barak

A. Recorded in Judges
   1. The actual story is in chapter 4
   2. Deborah's reflection on it is in chapter 5

B. The characters
   1. Jabin of Hazor
   2. Sisera his captain
   3. Deborah, who is functioning as judge
   4. Barak, the reluctant leader of the Israeli army
   5. Heber the Kenite, an almost-neutral party
   6. Jael, wife of Heber, who knew how to wield a mean hammer

C. The plot
   1. Jabin despoils Israel
   2. Deborah gets a message from the Lord
   3. She calls upon Barak to lead the people in their own defense
   4. Barak won't do so unless she goes with him
   5. They go to battle and rout the forces of Hazor
   6. Sisera takes refuge in a "neutral zone"
   7. Jael hides him and then kills him

II. The Unanswered Questions

A. Why was a woman in this place of responsibility?
   1. No man was readily available, which is a poor commentary on men
   2. Barak may have been typical (behind most women who dominate lies a man who won't lead)
   3. But there may have been another reason
      a. Appears Jabin and Sisera preyed on women (Judg. 4:6–7, 11, 30)
      b. God may have raised up a woman to deliver from power that preyed on women (Jabin may

have been able to prey on women because men were so weak)

B. Did Jael do right in killing Sisera?
   1. Note the locale reference—in the tent, not in the open
   2. There is a sense in which he asked for it
   3. It appears she did what had to be done; there was no one else to do it
   4. Had it not been for her act, there might not have even been a Mary

C. These facts may account for the order of names in Hebrews, and the association with women

III. The Lessons of Faith

A. Faith: hearing what God has said and believing it enough to act upon it

B. Lesson 1: Barak lost out on the blessing the Lord had for him through lack of faith. Deborah went with him, and he was the loser for not going by faith

C. Lesson 2: To Barak's credit, he went ahead and did what he had to do on the basis of the word of God to another person
   1. This is the first instance in Hebrews 11 where the person involved didn't get a direct message from the Lord
   2. Barak's word from the Lord came through Deborah
   3. He obeyed it reluctantly, but he still obeyed it
      a. We get messages direct from the Lord in the Word, but we also get them through those who preach the Word
      b. We ought to obey the message through someone else unless it violates the Word (we are better off than Barak as we have a means of checking the message against the Word, which he could not do)
   4. Faith hears what God has said—even through others—and believes it enough to act on it

Conclusion:

Most who preach don't mean to cry for personal recognition, etc., but they do profess to be God's messengers. Every message ever preached demands some response of faith. Flat rejection of the message or its appeal without some biblical warrant qualifies as "un-faith."

By Faith: Jephthah

Hebrews 11:32

Introduction:

The days of the Judges were very crude, primitive days (cf. Judg. 11:1–6). Jephthah was the son of a prostitute. He was taken into his father's house to be raised. He came into conflict with the birth sons and fled from them. He was surrounded by a bunch of rowdies ("vain"). He is a strange character with a strange story, who appears to be a strange addition to Hebrews 11.

I. **The Story of Jephthah**
   - A. Probably the only judge in a portion of Israel
   - B. They were being oppressed by the Ammonites
     1. His brethren came and called for him to represent or lead them
     2. The invitation automatically included his "rowdies"
   - C. He agreed to do so only on certain conditions (Judg. 11:9)
   - D. He entered into controversy with the Ammonites (Judg. 11:12–27)
   - E. He then went to war against Ammon (Judg. 11:28ff.)
   - F. In the process of all this, he made a vow to God (Judg. 11:30–31)
   - G. He was successful in battle (Judg. 11:33)
   - H. His own people turned against him (on a pretext) and the familiar story of the speech pattern took place (Judg. 12:1–7)

II. **The Strange Vow of Jephthah (Judg. 11:30–40)**
   - A. Appears that he offered his daughter as a sacrifice to the Lord (the language will certainly fit that idea—Judg. 11:37–40)
   - B. It is impossible to reconcile this with his knowledge of Scripture shown throughout the story (Judg. 11:15–22) as God had clearly, repeatedly forbidden such sacrifices
   - C. It is also difficult to reconcile this with his frequently shown knowledge of God's dealings with men
   - D. There is another possible answer (Judg. 11:31)
     1. The same Hebrew word rendered "and" can also be rendered "or" (and is frequently used that way)
     2. Thus: "shall surely be the LORD's, or I will offer it up for a burnt offering"

3. This fits the details just as well and avoids the problem of human sacrifice
    a. She was given to the Lord for tabernacle service to be a perpetual virgin
    b. This was a big issue in Israel—she would then not qualify to have a son who could prove to be the Messiah
4. This would also fit the actual language of the vow which is masculine—"himsoever cometh forth . . . I will offer him up for a burnt offering"
5. He actually could have gotten out of offering his daughter on this basis had he wished

III. Why Is Jephthah Included Here?

A. He does nothing more than a lot of others did

B. This vow is the one thing that distinguishes him
1. He vowed a vow
2. It didn't come out as he wished
3. He knew the Scriptures (Num. 30:2)
4. He lived by his vow
    a. Even though he could have wormed out of it
    b. Even though it involved a great cost to him

C. He heard the word of the Lord (shown over and over again) and believed it enough to act on it even though it involved something of tremendous personal cost

Conclusion:

The Hebrews doubtlessly had a problem with obedient faith right at this point, even as we have a problem with what happened. They tended to turn back when the cost got high. We tend to turn back when the cost gets high. What is it costing you to hear the Word and believe it enough to act on it? A lot of our disobedience, stunted growth, etc., stems from this area, and that is why I believe Jephthah is included in the list.

The Adventures of David

Hebrews 11:32

Introduction:

In interpreting Scripture, always try to determine what those who received the message would have heard (this will keep you from some extreme interpretations). In this case, it isn't so easy because there is so much said about David. But there seems to be one area that is special.

I. Identifying the Aspects of David's Faith

A. Many of the ten items listed in the following verses pertain to him

B. One in particular is attached to him (Ps. 144:10); he is delivered "from the hurtful sword"—through faith

II. Exploring the Stories Involved

David escaped the edge of the sword on at least three occasions that are notable.

A. Against Goliath who planned to behead him (1 Sam. 17:15–58)

B. In regard to Saul

1. God took His hand off Saul and rejected him
2. David was chosen to be Saul's successor long before Saul was dead
3. The victory over Goliath brought David into prominence
4. There was growing friction between them as Saul sensed that David was gaining prominence
5. Saul made several specific tries on David's life
   a. 1 Samuel 18:9–11
   b. 1 Samuel 19:1
6. In every case, David escaped the edge of the sword

C. In regard to the rebellion of Absalom (2 Sam. 15)

1. It was Absalom's avowed purpose to kill him (2 Sam. 17:1–3)
2. Through a variety of means, he escaped the edge of the sword

III. Examining the Stories Involved

A. There is more than meets the eye in each case

1. He escaped the edge of the sword
2. The manner in which he did so is important
3. It is more than God's preservation

B. Notice
   1. In the case of Goliath he escaped the edge of the sword by triumphing over him
      a. In spite of disparity
      b. With completely inadequate resources
   2. In the case of Saul, he not only escaped the edge of the sword, but he was willing to wait on God's purposes and timing (even to the point of sparing Saul on two occasions when he could have killed him—1 Sam. 24–26)
   3. In the case of Absalom, he not only escaped the edge of the sword, he triumphed over the situation to the point that he grieved over the death of the one who sought his own death

IV. Applying the Stories Involved

A. Definition of faith—hearing God and believing Him enough to act on what He has said

B. David had heard God, and we know when and where (1 Sam. 16:12–13)

C. As a result of hearing God and believing Him enough to act on what He had said
   1. He tackled a task far too big for him and easily brought it off (God had promised him the throne—there was nothing that could happen to him—he was invincible)
   2. He patiently waited for what had been promised and would not lift up his hand against Saul, allowing God to take care of the matter
   3. He did not seek vindication on Absalom—he knew he was somewhat to blame—but waited on God to work vengeance on his enemies

Conclusion:

There is so much to learn here.

Courage—When God promises something, it will come to pass no matter what, and you can act on it and take on any Goliath in your life.

Patience—When God has promised something, you can wait for it to happen, not forcing issues that belong to Him.

Compassion—When God has promised something, you can leave the righting of wrongs to Him in full confidence that He will care for what needs to be done.